# TURNING INTO ART

# VIVEKA SAHASRANI

For my Dad,

For leading me towards the art I am.

# Contents

# Contents

# Contents

This book is for those
Who felt art saved them
When no one else did

# Acknowledgements

Thank you Mom and Weirdo for believing me all through my writing blocks.

Thank you Abhishek V Tundurwar for initiating this book and Hemanth Varma for the stunning cover page.

Turning into Art


*Through Emotions*

# 1. Truth

Truth is a lonely human
She was tortured to death
By her belief system
Rotting her body day and night.
Mourning at the late facts
She screamed louder than her heart
Asking him to save her life.
She pleaded the sky to send him soon.
Appeal turned into curse
And the night into light.

The virtue never appeared
But the death do
The truth died
Thinking her life is never true

This legend passed on
From generation to generation

People started talking about the painful death
Truth has gone through
But they never know
There is much more suffering than death

It is the self doubt, truth has gone through
Especially in the last minutes of her death
She could have pleaded herself
Instead of virtue
To save her soul!!

# 2. Truth about Truth

Fast forward 20 th century

This truth started to live inside our inhibitions
Trying to save her soul
It started hiding so much with time
That it happened to be invisible by now

People started getting mad
With self doubt
But the truth about truth is
There is nothing like proving it
For she was born to be herself
What is the need of conspiracy ?!

Yet no one believes in her

Because they need that late facts
Truth mourned at
Once upon a time.

# 3. Inhibitions

My first inhibition held me in
Not being a disappointment
To the people around

What if saying 'No' makes me rude
What if expressing myself makes me weak
What if the confidence behind "i can"
Makes me egoistic
What if my boundaries make me unapproachable
What if , What If

There are days with dual answers
Written in my head
There are days with internal fights
Tattooed forcibly on my heart
There are filters attached to my mouth
To lift the answers that are less defensive

Trying to be sane
I started losing sanity

It actually took me a while

To understand the difference between politeness and trying not to be a disappointment.

# 4. Perfection

When i try to crush my inhibitions at first place
It costs the perfection inside me
Maybe not the perfection
But at least the idea associated with it.

I don't know why the world runs behind
The word called 'Perfection'.
No one really knows it
We all live upon the idea of perfection
Perfect career
Perfect bodies
Perfect life
But no one knows
What is the perfect thing
Or who is the perfect person.
When i hear the word perfection,
And the talks given by those
Aimless intellectuals trying
to portray themselves as heroes.
The first thing that comes across my mind is
How far their life is distanced from that perfection
And do they think someone is leading a perfect life ?
If so , have they heard it from those perfectionists words?

Of Course, they won't!!

Because the answer is here
Those who define perfection in someones eyes
Knows what it costs to be there
and are, of course chasing their updated terms on 'perfection'.

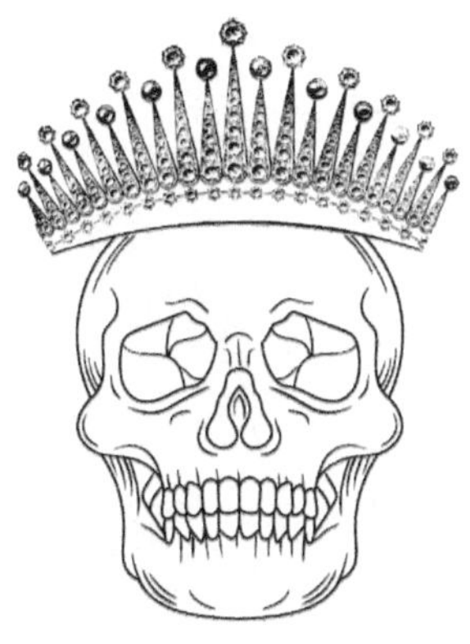

# 5. Differentiating things

If there is a simply complex thing
We are neglecting for ages
It is Differentiating things

We live through a lot of things
Thinking it is something else

We will be in a company
Thinking it is love

We will be in a career
Thinking it is passion

We will be in wrong guidance
Thinking it is parenting

We will be in the same place
Thinking it is where we belong to

# 6. Belongingness

You know what belongingness feels like ?
It feels like
The heart catching the soul
within its fist space
And surprisingly it is cozy,
not narrow

Belongingness doesn't need parameters
It needs that little magic we carry in our eyes
Every time we came across it
It makes you dwell like a mad man
Reading the rainbow in a desert

The moment you come across the
Feeling of belongingness
The person whom you are seeking for
And the person who is seeking is same

And suddenly all the process
Makes sense that
How you read the word called purpose of life
On a random evening
And here you are, this day, this moment

Holding that word unto your life already

# 7. Purpose

Everytime i look at the sky
I wonder if it is god's finest canvas
He ever built for himself
But what was his first inspiration
To become an artist.

I think it is the question of a peasant
Before turning into a nomade
And walking away from home
To find a new purpose.
But here is the problem
The idea associate with purpose is easy
But the complexity in understanding it
Take the lifetime credits to solve.

And here is our lonely peasant
Walking through the deserts
And oceans
With one word called purpose
And when he is in his last hope
To find a way to reach his purpose.
He looked at the sky
Finding the courage to keep going.

I think that's the god's art inspiration
"To try one last hope
Till the journey is accomplished".

# 8. Courage

Courage isn't everything
We read in epics.
May be, It is to walk away
And listen to your footsteps
While they scare you to death.
And then there will be
another announcement
"Walking away is easy,
But never looking back
Take everything outta you".

Days of Despair and
Nights aren't much darker
Than the insomnia
But it isn't done yet
There will be two wolves
Inside your brain
Fighting each other
"One saying Screw it!
And other, what if?"
That's when you gotta
Look right into their eyes
And stand still.

That's it,
For that will wake you up
To your life time affirmation
"You are more than
Those wolves screwing inside your brain"
"You are more than those scariest footsteps
You walked through"
"You are more than your uncertain days and nights.

Courage is all along the way
Right from "walking away to waking up".

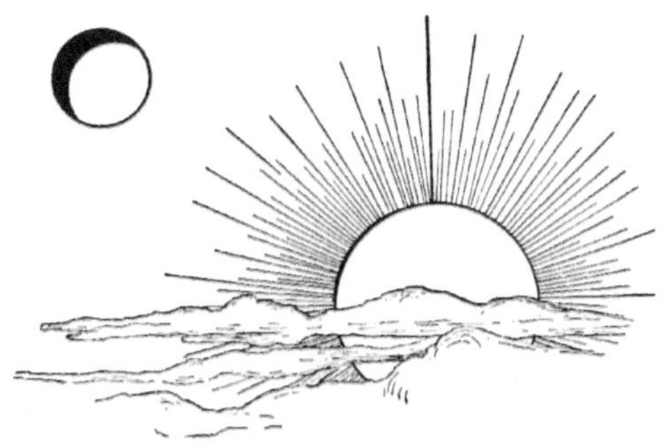

# 9. Last Apology

So i picked up
That last apology i have,
to offer to the World
And i offered it to myself
For playing all long
To cope up with the world

Don't you think
You owe an apology too
For flipping your magnificent story
And normalising it
to people understandability
And to look best in their eyes.

Forget about it
You need not be user friendly.
For you are not an app
But a breathing person
With an unpredictable brain
And uncertain emotions
Like the monsoon wind.

Wake up

Clear your mind
For everything
You have lost today
You have tomorrow
To build yourself up.
Because you aren't a thing
To be lost.
You are that fire
Which burns outta ashes
After halting it
for many 'one last times'.

# 10. Stay Awake

Everytime you let
Someone influences you.
Remember
It is always a war
To be accepted
Either a rule or a personality.
Sometimes from a group of people
other times from a worldwide entity.
It could be from one person
And their multiple favourite conversations
Or Ewww, grow up ?! from your foe.

I wish you will stay awake
Before taking a choice
Without bearing consequences.
I wish you will stay awake
Before getting inspired
Without learning their story.
I wish you will stay awake
Before accepting the win
And neglecting the loss.
I wish and wish
That one enlightened Awakening.

Before you lost yourself

In their drama

They played themselves to be the main character.

• 21 •

# 11. You deserve to be loved!

Once, you shivered in fear all the night
And when I asked you, what happened?
You said it's nothing, but a bad dream.
And slept back, still shivering.

What you know is
I haven't slept that night
but what you never know is
I am spending night after night
Thinking how to make you feel safer again.

Everytime when you feel your suffering is invalid.
I wish I was there holding you.
Everytime, your mind keeps questioning
Your worth, I wish I could frame your strength.
Everytime you feel your emotions making you a weak person.
I wish i was there telling you it's okay to be human
Everytime your mood, swings from high to low
I wish you know i got your back.

Because humans like you deserve to be loved
In the times of anxiety , especially when your mind keeps on

saying

You deserved to be punished with isolation.

# 12. Be Safe place to your loved ones

If there is something
you could do
to save the world,
Be the safest place to a person
You meet every single day.
Because life isn't fair to any of us,
not even a single of us.
That doesn't mean
We are going to end
this unfair game either,
instead we fight,
we fight for ourselves, our dreams
and to whatever we believe in
and that's what life is meant to be,
Maybe ?!

But make this point clear.
If you can't be the safest place
to your dear ones,
they tend to run for random strangers
Hoping to find their home
Well, now that's the biggest challenge,

Because you know,
if someone dearest to them
Can't be their safe place ,
How can you expect that stranger to be? or this entire world
to be ?
And that's where they will get ditched
Fair enough ?!

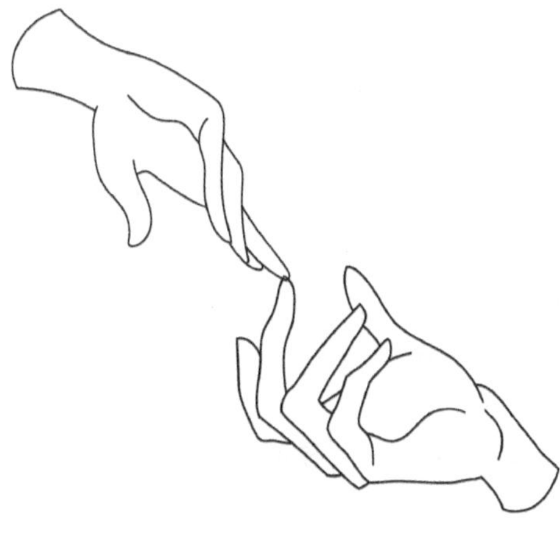

# 13. Silencing your Soul?

Do we need a thunderstorm
To feel safer again ?

What it feels like
To silence a soul
And Commanding it
To be specific
And to act in a specific way

Soul itself has a language
We unfortunately have to understand.
It haunts sometimes
And it's a mere friend the other time
There is nothing like
It's going to be that of your idol's
Whom you worship to become

Of course there are courses
laying everywhere around
To mold your soul as you wanted to.
May be at the cost of your insecurities.

But once this soul started shutting itself

From everything else
All it need is a storm to feel safer again
The chaos that are equal
To the chaos going on inside!

# 14. What would you do?

I would like to ask you
What are you going to do
If you are a normal human ?

I accept it
You all have a story
And you assume yourself
To be the Hero in it.
And running all the way
To be one.
So now let's assume it opposite

What are you going to do ?
If you are just a human
With Grief , Anger , Ego and Fear
And you accept them all
Before it is too late
And ready to rectify them.

Are you going to apologise
Your sibling for taking
Away his property wrongly

Are you going to fall on
Your knees and cry your heart
In Front of your loved one
Till they understand
Your love towards them ?

What are you going to do ?
Because Death bed
is your last confession
You have with yourself.
And it doesn't contain
Money , fame or your run all the way

But the wrongs you have done
And the regrets you hold
To be the hero you assume yourself to be.
But it is too late
To rectify them.

So awake when you are alive
And answer yourself
What are you going to do ?

# 15. Emotions

Do you still think
People need patterns
To the way they feel ?
I have heard a lot of stories
Contrary to the way
They are shown to the world.

That military man
Who invaded wars single handedly
Died at the loss of his loved one.
It's not always the strength
We wear in our eyes
But the softness
We clasp dearly in our hearts.

Do you know?
people who aren't afraid of death
Are afraid of the emotions
They carry.
And once they find the safest home
for their emotions
The death feels scary to them
Contrast aren't they ? Yet in a single heart!

People says with age
We become strong
But they never dare to accept
Physical strength is inversely proportional
To mental strength.
That's why one deep cry as a boy
turns into 100 days of silent screams of a man.

Are we afraid of emotions too much ?
Or Are we selling souls to catch brain patterns ?

# 16. Emotional thesis

People say this world is for
Those who speak
But what about the poets
Who sobs inside their words
Does their silence matters
If no one ever reads their poem?

It isn't always about the lack of words
to explain what a person going through
But the trust they have with the world,
It isn't always up to the bars.

When did your brain started
To invade your heart?
With the words saying
"Forget about it!!
Even if they understand
They won't understand"

Sadness sometimes is fatal
We cannot escape it
And cannot face it either
Instead we make it as a part of life

But you know how it feels like
It feels like the ocean accepted its waves
But the twist is, when you breath waves
Tornado isn't a separate ritual.
It is always within!

So I wont say let's open up
For this tornado gulps us together.
Instead i will let you know
I am here with you
Like i always do
Silently watching the storm, to pass
As it came.

# 17. Sadness isn't that bad

Sadness isn't that bad
If we embrace it differently.

Have you wondered ?
How 5.00 AM emptiness
Urges you to come out of the room,
And watch the sun rising slowly
Like the hope inside you,
When you are a fading sunset.

Have you observed ?
How you stopped
From your long life run,
To take a deep breath,
And that air felt different.

Have you listened ?
How that same song
Which you are listening
For years now,
Beats different today
to align your chaos.

Have you cherished it?
How your best friend cried along,
Instead of slamming the doors
Like others do
And you felt less lonely
With the world.

Sadness isn't that bad
For it explains us
What comes along and
How to understand things
In a different way
Just like the art do
May be that's why
We feel art understand our sadness.
But is it art that understands our sadness ?
Or the artist who understand
The differences differently.

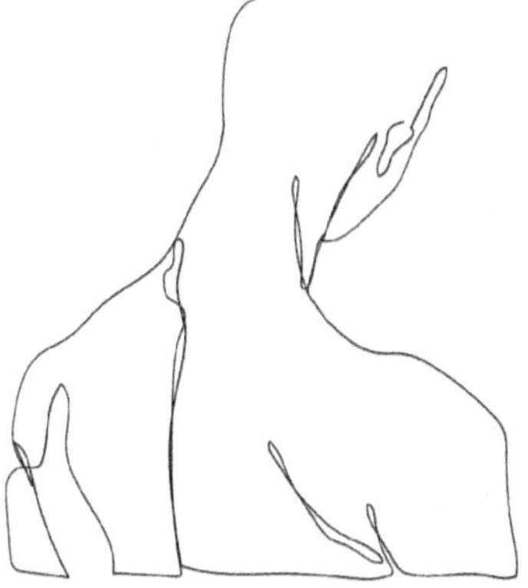

# 18. Hey Art!

Is it you?
Is it me? Is it us?
How do you know?
Hundred years back
That i am going to feel void someday
And you are created
Exactly to fill those spaces.

Colours aligned
And they change
Without changing
The patches that artist
Forgot to fill the colours with,
Is intentional.

Art cannot be understood all the time
Because we try to seek a rainbow in it .
But it is for the colour blind people
Who failed to express their emotion
And one day they stare at a painting
And understand themselves.
Oh! This is why I felt this that day.

You know what?
Our heart is layered
With emotions
And most of the time
These emotions come out black and blue
Which are very hard to understand
And unpleasant to bear.

And there we start
Opening up to the art
Because there is a person
Centuries ago
Who has seen it coming!!

What Else is a real comfort
If it isn't being understood
Without uttering a word!!

• 40 •

# 19. Art talks

People talk about success stories
But art talks about the real stories
The stories that are disappointing ….
The stories that are too disappointing for the authorities
To write them in an authorised way.

The stories that are troublesome
To talk with a filtered mouth of supremacy
The stories that are tried to be hidden
Before they could lighten up someone's mind.

The stories that are broken
To be fixed back again
The stories that make a human
To be a human and nothing else
The stories of pain
The stories of love
The stories of obsession
The stories of desperation.

These stories are encrypted in
The vocals of a musician
The Paint brush of an artist

The Heart of a poet
And the eyes of a dancer.
And they live on
Till there is passion in our soul
And magic in our thoughts.

# 20. Unleash yourself

Some poems talk to us today
Some poems talk to us
Days after we read them
Some poems talk to us
When we write them
Some poems talk to us
When we read them over
Some poems talk to us
When we narrate them
Some poems talk to us
When we listen to them
Poems, they always talk
Until we listen
Poems, they always listen
Until we talk.

"Poems , they are
That fragile connection
We have with ourselves
Waiting for the conversation to happen"
- Unleash yourself

# 21. Poetry is my Love language

Poetry,

What a strangest love language

I tryna communicate with this world.

Words after words

Analogies after Analogies

Poems after poems.

I look myself in a better way

For loving this world

Little more than before.


I write deepest sense of sadness

Thinking these words

Somewhere, are going to hug

A lonely stranger

Suffering from Sadness

And make her feel better

Because someone understood

Her misery through these poems.


I write poems

For a boy bullied by his own friends

Or mocked by his office colleagues

For being a normal dude .
I wonder if he understand
Normal dude are so special
That they are admired in poems.

I write vintage love
For that oldman
Who was left in an old age home.
When nothing comforts him but love
I wish these lines narrate the stories
Of his good young days with his wife.
And comforts him with a smile.

I wish my poems comfort you too
In someway like
the wind comforts the air
And Rain comforts the Sea
Even if they aren't much noticed
I wish they had an impact in one heart
In this big world.

# 22. Till death we do art



Have you bothered looking black,
while admiring a rainbow?
And a lunar eclipse,
While staring at the moon?
It is always art
That let you love things
In black and blue.

I listened to a poetess saying
"Give me the pain
My words can bear
For i will pen it down
it isn't mine anymore".
What can hold her darkness
with open arms, If it isn't art ?

Once i started painting my wall
It isn't a wall for me, It is emptiness!
For i hold void and art like twins
I wanted this emptiness to be colourful.
With every colour , i painted
I have my waves of anxiety
Settled in peace .

"Wall turned into starry night
But waves are back into scarry night"
I smiled thinking
"What else a sea can do
If it isn't moon phases
That are modulating these WAVES?"

That's when i hold back my paint brush
Affirming 'til death we do art.
It aint a choice , it's freedom from WAVES.

# 23. Empaths need to be found!

So what makes you
Stop creating art ?
I asked my Artist friend.

Well!
It's making me
To adopt the sadness
From the world
She replied
You know, i can walk
Around the world twice,
Lonely like a poem
But you know,
The emotion it carries ?
It is the biggest deal.

Poem is just a set of words
Until someone adopts
the emotion, it contains
And I , like that poem
Can be a lonely world wanderer
Until someone

Explain me what loneliness feels like!

This is what
Art making me
To feel everything around,
In order to let it flow from my veins.

But Unfortunately this heart
Isn't a water bearer
While the world is an ocean of sadness!

She said
Leaving her paintbrush in my hands
And losing herself to the art
'That was placed in the corner of the museum
And gone unnoticed for years'
Just like the sadness in the world .
"May be WORLD needs Empaths
To be found".

# 24. To feel my heart safer

I often get lost in poetry.
Somewhere someone is
Getting bullied
I feel it in my skin and bones.
And when my favourite poet
Dwells in every word
He scribbles.
I listen to him within
Those words.

The trees grow on purpose,
The birds sing on purpose and
We live on purpose according to me.
I like checking out on silent souls
The one who seeks silence
Away from parties.
The ones who look at the moon
And pour their hearts.
The ones who don't talk
But have an entire world inside.

I hate intelligence
Because before

Everything else
It creates greed of owning.
It questions the magic.
It questions the difference.
I want the world to celebrate differences.
Instead of questioning them.
Some freaking things
Should be just they are
Without intelligence interrupting them.
Coolest things aren't cool for me.
When a person is dying alive
Because of your intelligence label.
You are still a freaking demon
According to me.

I often get lost in poetry
Like all poets do
Certainly to feel my heart safer one day.

• 55 •

# 25. Freedom

If you have to pick my heart,
you have to search for
The most abandoned ways possible.

The ways that are no more
In the pages of literature
The ways that are no longer
Understood by modern poets
The ways that are no harder
Written in human language.

I walk all the gardens
Yet no flowers knows my existence
I fly all though the sky
And no birds know my muse
I swim all over the oceans
And no fish remember my plight.

I dwell in the colours of the fallen flowers
That arent plucked from their mothers
I rest in the freedom of a cage
Every time a bird met her wings
I dive in the deepest end of sailors possibility

When a fish breathe through it gills.

My existence is as simple as i look
And as hard as i exist.
And you still tryna seek my heart ?!!!

Turning into Art


*Through Body*

# 26. Trapped Under Human Skin

Most of the days
She feels like
She was trapped
Under this human skin

While she wanted
To be a melody
Flowing around
In the woods

She, the wildflower
Belongs to the wild
Not your bouquet
Or your vase

She isnt a mere human emotion
To be someone's belonging
But a goddamn sunset of her own
Which never sets as it appears.

Turn the globe around
You will see her rise!!

# 27. Anxiety through Body

There is something
more than mind
about emotions
It is body.

These emotions tend to talk to you
And when you refuse to listen them
They tend to show up on your bodies
In the most uncomfortable ways.

The race in your tummy
And the rush in your heart
The weight on your head
And tenderness on your skin
The Length of your breath
And the tension on your muscles.

Why does your hands feel the urge
To hide your face all the time?
Why do you tap your leg continuously
To feel less lonely, until you walk from that place
What is that feeling squeezing your heart
That you wanted to walk so fast ?

Why are you biting your tongue
Every time you feel stressed ?

What are you up to ?
When your body trying to confess something?
Which home are you running from to feel safer?

Stand there right now
And listen to it
Sometimes solution lies in not running away
At Least from yourself!!!

# 28. Body and confusion

People say depression is a mind thing
But why do you think
People isolate themselves
Everytime they come across
The uncertainties inside their mind.

I think it is really hard to explain
Everytime someone
Generalise the word depression to laziness
Stop being lazy
Try to find solutions
Stop being lazy
Try to make friends
I hope you learn theories
Before you shoot the assumptions.

Depression isn't just
Rolling into the bed
It is your body treating you like a refugee
And you wanted to find a new home
A home that is so new to you
That you roll into it
Before being caught by someone

Saying Hey! You don't belong here.

Depression isn't just
Laying in the darkness
It is to face the light lighter than the feather
But heavier on your skin
With the questions written all over
In an invisible ink.

Depression isn't just
Isolating themselves
In the room
But that confused body wanting
To curl up to its least
To make sure it is there
And it can never be taken away from them.

Depression isn't the assumptions
Associated with it
But your body seeking help
Aligned with the messed up emotions
Before it enters your life.
**Sort it out!!**

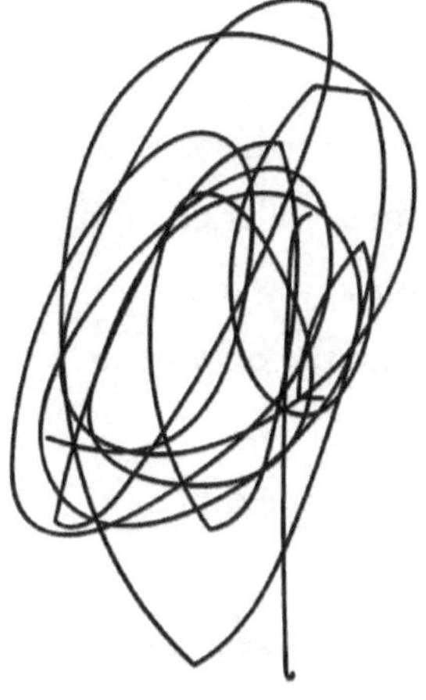

# 29. Body Crisis

The crisis body goes through
Is the biggest emotional roller coaster.
If we define this crisis as a war
You and your body are the opponents.
You battle so fiercely
As if you wanted to end the other.

Sometimes the body acts like a traitor
It listens to the situations
You are walking through externally and
starts bothering you at its best
And you, you aren't an easy human either
So you feed every toxicity your body hates
Saying it relieves your stress.

But at the end of the war
You are no more without your body
And your body is no more with you
You are together in this
You have to pamper each other
Because no one can enter
That personal space
You share with each other.

The pain is mutual
And so does the healing.

Be kind to your body
And so the body will!!

# 30. Body and Self Harm

Attention!!!
This is your body speaking
Its 3 AM in the morning
With hatred preoccupied
In your mind.

Your emotions enraged
Holding the fist so desperately
To punch something around
Your teeth are clenched
Hard enough to stop your biggest cry
And the legs kicking the floor
Trying to stop this revolving world.

No one is around,
Yet i am here with you and being you
And ready to be your victim
But let me clear few things
You never know
Especially when your conscious is
Blinded by your emotions
Here you go,
You know what I am made of ?

I am made of the patience and pain
I am not that mere emotion
You trying to exhibit on me.

I am both the survival and consistency
It took me more than 2 weeks to become tissue
4 weeks to build the nervous system
5 weeks to turn into a bud
6 weeks to feel the heartbeat
8 weeks to align the inch growth
12 weeks to grow hair and nails
28 weeks to be responsive
And this goddamn life till today
To stand like this.

You still think, you have the authority to hurt me
Over a mere emotion ?

# 31. Seek the Beauty

Look at your acne
Clean your skin properly, why are you ignoring this
O my god , you put on weight these days
I think you should go on with a proper diet
Have you noticed your lips turned black
I think you need balm
You are less than the weight you should be
Try attending nutritionist sessions.

My Dear free advisers
I washed my skin too much
That it started falling off my face
Yes, I put on weight for allowing
The body types to define me
And the curves to make me beautiful
Now that it exceeded its limit
I cannot stop it
Yes my lips turned into bulky black
For abusing the seasonal difference
They carry naturally.
And oh my lightweight,
I hope your brain carries the same
And for your kind information

It's my genetics that makes me light
Neither my food , nor my negligence.

Next time try being comfortable with your bodies
Before looking at someone's differences differently
I hope you go to the day
You start accepting your bodies are flawful
From someone's eyes.
And start seeking the beauty it is.

# 32. Be that way

Big heights of strength
Comes from not trying
To hide your vulnerability.

You have to understand
That you need to
Normalise yourself
To you.

The way you feel
The way you react
The way you think
The way you look

We are highly
Caught up in
Feeling how they thought us
To feel about certain things
And redefined ourselves from who we are.

Maybe it helps in someway
But not at the cost of ruining
our sanity.

But by Normalising
our own bodies,
The changes they go through,
The emotions they feel,
And the way they look.
There is no way
That someone
Can use it against you
Or to bully you.

Because
You are well aware
Of who you are.
And by accepting it
Your insecurities
Stop being weapons
In other's hands.

# 33. Bodies and memories

What if i say
We add memories
To our bodies
Some are intentional and love labels
Some are symbols of hatred
Some are visible and louder
While others are sealed in "Unheard"

Can you see
That biggest scar on your hand ?
It is from an accident you met a few years ago
With your best friend next to you.
But Instead of worrying the next move
You laughed at each other.

But that wrong touch you had in your office
Isn't visible to naked eyes
Yet it feels like the feeling
You wanted to puke out of your brain
Yet it happens to be in your mind every single day.

I would like to know the muse
Behind your tattoo

It must be the most important thing after all
But i also wanted to know the story
Behind the same tattoo
When that muse left you like you never matter
It must be the story
Narrated to those
Who feels like listening to them.

I wanted to listen to the art you are, in both phases.

# 34. Blooming on bare skin

What is the primary way
To lead a life?
And how do we know
Is it right or wrong ?
I used to ask.

Nature leads us the way
And that's why we are
gifted with rains
And punished with floods
To balance our filthy minds
I was answered by a Naturalist

And only if Nature can lead me
I would like to observe it closely
I want Flowers, The Part of this nature
to lead me
I want them to bloom on my bare skin
And get faded every single day.
To remind me nothing lasts
but everything blooms the next day.

I want them to fall one by one

Whenever i struggle with self love
For they explain running away from myself
Is nothing but creating a void in my existence.

I want them to change colours
Everytime i bottle up my emotions
I want these colours to Scream
"life is all about experiencing emotions
Yellow, Orange, Brown"
For the differences are their beauty.

I want them to represent myself
Inside out to walk this life
For i am too much polished by
This Human race Racing
To know what is right and what is wrong!

# 35. Body

Science says
We become a whole different
Person for every seven years
But where does that old traits go
Especially those intense roller coasters
The desperation, the obsession and the thirst.

Sometimes we are ashamed of ourselves
For the emotions we go through.
We feel like our hearts are
The filthiest Battle grounds
To get betrayed upon.
In the first phase
We stand in front of ourselves
To fight the strongest opponent ever
These wars are not less than the world wars
For we dwell upon a lot of worlds inside
We tear these worlds until they flow like tears
We Cut them bleed and squeeze them out
To scream and scream to talk these things about.

And these battles happen
Until we forgive ourselves.

Forgiving isn't a process
That happens
With one strongest sentence
We say and hear constantly.
It won't happen
With one good conversation
Or one healing therapy.

But ......!
But it isn't a myth either
Just like the body forgiving
And rebuilding itself
For every seven years.
We have to forgive ourselves
Through our mind , intuition and conscious
We have to learn and relearn,
Inorder to be honest with ourselves
And building a new set of consciousness
Isn't that easy.

For this body needs
120 days to start from
The minute part of its least.
How about healing our inner worlds
To be a new bloomed person again?
Definitely is a matter of consistency

But to move through the journey
we have to start that step anyway,
With one step, a time!!

# 36. Learn from your bodies

When you try to heal
You need to be prepared for the process
Entangled with healing.

First it relies on clotting
And restricting the healing part
To not to go back to what is hurting
and ruining things that are no where
Related to it.

and then it proceeds through flushing out the repaired,
What is unnecessary and foreign to it.
The hardest part about healing is
We grieve over the toxic parts
Because we are attached to
Newness and mystery.
Simply human traits of enthusiasm
Trying to figure out what it holds.

Once you start
Being comfortable in your shoes
The new beginning will be layered
And the beginnings will be dispersed

In such a way that the wound will be closed forever
Sometimes a wound leaves the body leaving a scar ,
With it's a hallmark of new beginning.

Somewhere our body owns and owes
'Mine' feeling all through itself
For it never leaps over any steps
Or leave the process impatiently.

- Learn from your body

# 37. Treating the body like an art

Vulnerability hits different
It doesn't need a foggy day
To push you away from the sunlight
But your will to close the curtains.

So next time
When you feel like
You are having a bad hair day
Or a saggy stomach
With labels on your skin
Or hair under your chin
Take a moment to celebrate this creation
Try to observe this art clearly
Before accepting the flaws imposed on it.
For greatest arts that are abandoned
that day in the history
It isn't for their ugliness but
For the lack of eyes to witness their beauty.

Promise me looking at the cosmos in the night sky
Everytime a seasonal change approaches your skin
Your veins are the roots a tree carries beautifully

And the marks on your eyes are as same as
The lines on the petals to make the flower more aesthetic
Your grey hairs are vintage leaves changing colours with time.

• 89 •

For your body is a creation
Growing yourself to understand it, is all the beauty it carries.

# 38. Love note to your body

Dear body
We are companions for a long way now
And i am sorry for imposing labels on you
For abusing you every time there is a new standard
In body shapes and career growth.
I know i am working for a long time restlessly
I regret saying this , my darling body!!
I have been really harsh on you.

Sometimes, i imagine
If being harsh on someone else
Makes me punishable under law,
what punishment i would be under
If there is a statement for abusing you?
I should have listened to you
Instead of the people.
For you are the one
Who is with me
In the times, no one has an idea upon.

You, been looking at me , growing with me
And responding to all my emotions
What a breathtaking witness you are

For my pride and prejudice
Thank you for your patience
In the moments of breakdown
I love you, Just the way you are.

# 39. Celebrating the body

Ocean and waves
They talk to me everytime
I walk through the beach on my bare foot
We play together
Sometimes I build the sand forts
And these waves,
they are naughty enough to push my fort
And before I caught them insanely
They wet my clothes and laugh away
We cherish those childhood friends we are.
We have grown up now
They give me their longest hug
For our today's are tomorrow's yesterdays
And can never be the same.

Everytime I move closer to them
These waves start aligning from my toes to head
To celebrate the person I am
They hear my heartbeat
Mend my breath
Settle in the corners of my skin,
To the Ears and hair
Everytime they touch my ears

They drop stories running around them
Sometimes these stories are lonely
Other times they are muses.
But the talk with the ocean is never ending
And every time I wave, the waves, a bye!
They look at me like I never return their love
Yet they leave part of them with me
The sand stuck on my head
And the salt waxed on my skin
The seashells in my pocket
And their narrations in my heart.

# 40. Time ain't going anywhere

Time ain't going anywhere
Until you do.
Take a moment to breathe.
And slay those yoga moments.
Make time for yourself.

Take care of your mind
Take care your body
Take care of your life.

Dues come back
Regrets come back
Challenges come back
Expectations come back.
And then there is this moment
When you look back
Unto your life.

You will feel proud
For being consistent in self talk
And those affirmations that keeps you moving
For understanding your body

And observing it closely,
On how is it responding
Everytime you face certain situations.

Your body will reward you for this
Just because the response is slower
That doesn't mean
The body isn't listening to your moves.
Be conscious that you are witnessing your moves from inside.

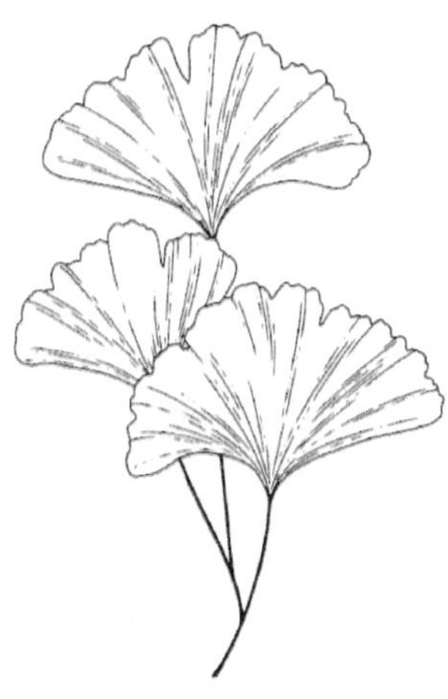

Turning into Art


*Through Life*

# 41. Dreams

What a lonely thing it is
To keep the dreams alive.
Even if you have a person
To cherish your dreams with
It still, is a lonely thing.

At the end of the day
The world will be on your shoulders.
Win or lose
It's completely yours.

I think Dreams are that fire
We somehow encrypted in our hearts
This fire can help the person
To survive and write the future.
But only the wise knows,
Introducing fires into our lives
Is nothing but intruding death on our will
There is no looking back
And this pyre
Has no difference between you
And a world champion
One moment of negligence

Can turn you into ashes.

But what's more interesting about this fire is
It can make the corpses narrate their stories.

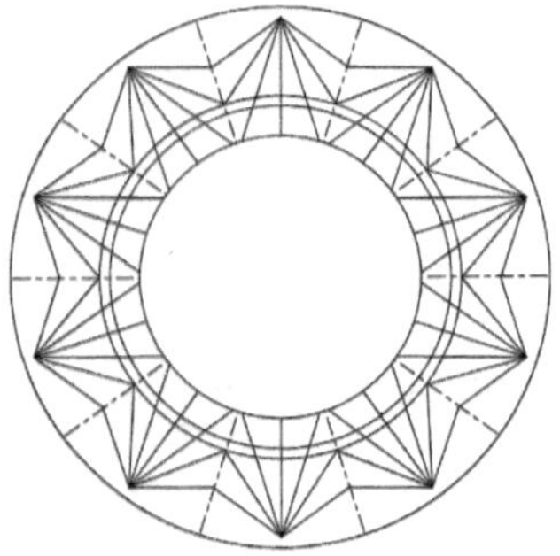

# 42. Passion

I think there is this slightest differences between
Obsession and passion
Obsession ask to catch the kite
While the passion remains us
To keep the kite flying.

I wonder what god might be feeling
Especially when he added the word passion
Unto human stories.
Because it redefines the survival game.

I got to learn about a passionate photographer
And an obsessed cameraman all together
in a single human.

When i ask him
What is he still running for ?
When he had everything fallen into places already.

Some things are for ourselves, he replied.
Neither for the money nor for the recognition
we simply do them for just the way they are
And for me it is to learn human stories

And capturing them twice
Once with in my heart
And other with the camera.

For these stories are with me
When I am nothing
To I understand the meaning of nothingness.
These are that bookmarked parts
I am living for!!

# 43. Wanderer

I am always a wanderer
Searching for some meaning
But the difficulty lies in
Searching for something unknown.

I wonder
What defines happiness and sadness?
Unless you feel
That slightest squeeze
In your stomach
And able to differentiate
If they are butterflies
Or goddamn caterpillars.

That's makes me wonder
What if every feeling we feel
Is a poet's muse on
What a beautiful place this world is
And trying to explain the beauty
He added language to his emotions
If not how do we even know the beauty of it,
This beautifully!!

Most of the times these poets
Lends me their mind
To seek answers in the poetry
For questions I never know I am searching for.

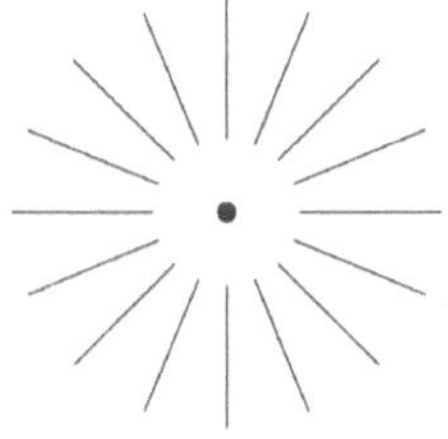

# 44. Poet's Muse

Poet is a muse of his own madness
For he believes Everything is alive
With or without moment
Tendency of never movable stone
Have its very story
with never ending river
For Every droplet passing in the river
In its own destination
Touches the stone which is standing still
Stone is immovable yet it is movingpart of its muse Is within
the droplet now
And half of the droplet Is damn dead
in the muse of stone

They are mutual and beautiful
The poet writing his madness
In the dawns , the waves , the muses and the skies
Its never ending -fight and love
To move immovable and to die lively
Everything oppositely within
and every moment
Poet is a muse of his own madness.

# 45. Into the wild

Ounce by ounce
I am falling in love,
To dance,
Matching the melody of air
Without music beat around
I am falling ,
To be away from human traces
And live in the woods
With a river flowing near by
I am falling
To look at the galaxy
Without light
And fill my hope
With the brightening stars.

I am falling
To fly away ,
back to mountains
Forests and darkness
Where survival happened
In its very beginning
And Definitely not this
Artificial intelligence ,

Lightning , self love demonstrators,
Influencers of some sort
Explaining why you should be like them.

Life and death should happen
Just like that
Without letting our soul to suffer
I mean what is the point of building
A mansion , if all you could do is
Regretting all your life
for turning a 500 year old tree's life
into your mansions door
Just for your own survival of 50 to 70 years maximum.

# 46. Celebration of life

Dazzling lights
Louder echos
Everyone is talking
So i found this corner
Away from the group
To sit and dream
I started staring out the glass door
And It was framed with fog.
To those who says
The night is young
I felt it then
Not in the party
But in the abandoned
Darkness outside.
What am I doing here ?
When all i need is, to feel alive
But this is not the life that feels lively.
And then he appeared
To be a tulip in the world of roses,
Feeding the stray dog.
The dogs seemed familiar to him
So do the wind dancing to his muse.
He looked back straight from the glass

Breaking that typical me
That's the moment after ages
I threw away my party heels
Running around the strays,
Feeling the chills of the wind
And Screaming
"The night is young
For those who celebrate it
Without bounds "
And That's entirely
"A life of celebration in one damn moment".

# 47. Loners

Loners have this tendency
To look life in small things
They stare at dead leaf
And can live for months
With out other communication
They touch the droplet
And feel the loneliness of sea
They walk on sand
And live the history of desert
There is nothing
That you could add more life to them
for your feel good helping nature or mercy
Becoz they either ask more or
just give up every human trace.
Don't ever promise them your time
If you can't make peace with their silence
They aren't your practicals
To show world how good you are
Or how amazingly talkative you are
Leave them alone
If you can't wait till they break their silence.

# 48. Wild Flower

She is a muse
Every time when melody embarks with music
She appears to be its soul
She is so soulful that
davinci started seeking beauty in her muse
Rather than the queen's face
to create monalisa.

She, is the moon
Every poet's first love and
every girl's secret keeper
She wans and waxes darkness
all long the cycle and stands still.

She is that wild flower
Tribal prayed years after years
to be blessed
only to cut it twice
After being blessed
She is the sunflower
Vincent longs to fade his art with
But bloomed after his death.

She is an echo of art
Which is so louder
To those who never seek it
And a lullaby
For those who crave it.

Because she is a woman of dreams
Who walks down and dawns fearlessly
To become everything and anything
Life throws at her.

# 49. Abundance

I love looking into people's lives
From their eyes.
All i wanted to do is
To feel the magic
They know about themselves.

Once i remember
Talking to a lady who sells incense sticks.
She holds magic in her eyes
Regardless the hurdles
She is going through.

When asked what's going on?

She settled on our veranda
Narrating her story like the best poets
In the world
Sometimes, i think
we can find greatest poets
Not in the books
But in the streets.

She said

Her life is a shooting star
For her children to wish upon
To make their dreams come true.
Her dreams, they are mermaids
That are too fairy to accomplish.
Her marriage is mirage
Caught in the desert
And her heart
It is sand,
that falls continuously
Everytime he lose the grip,
In a faith that nothing can empty a desert.

When i am thinking her stars might turn
Into waters.
She smiled at her abundance
In being a desert
And took the stars to next home
To sell the incense sticks.

# 50. Togetherness

Sun welcomed night,
Going back to his wife
Stars started giggling at the moon
and rain appeared
like an unwanted guest.
I, like that moon,
alone in the darkness,
was standing on the road
Away from the street goons.

Then this old couple
Appeared ,Holding hands
They seems to be
Living love poems
Written by every poet
In the world.

I followed this old couple
Only to disappear
From those goons
But the destiny
Welcomed me to
Witness love.

It isn't like a fantasy movie
Ordering the best food for her.
It is as simple as ordering food
And wait till she eats
Only to complete the left over.

The old man laughed at her
Like in mid 20's
For she is still not able
To complete the entire meal
After 40 years.
And she pretended to be
that mid young woman
With slight irritable silly smile.

I smiled there with my heart
For such big moment.

# 51. Treasure in existence

Empty rooms , Broken walls
Dirty curtains ,Gloomy webs
He seated in the same room
That he has been sitting for
The past 10 years.

Poor ? Nah
Abandoned ? Nope
What are you seeking
He was asked.

I am searching the treasure
He replied,
The same precious one
That i am seeking
For the past 10 years.
"It's her existence
And our togetherness
For 50 years".

For it is in this air and
It is new, every single day.
And so i seek it daily

Right in view of this balcony
And the plants , she planted
Which are trees now
The curtains she sewed
And the stories she narrated along.

Memories are the treasures
we live for, the old man said
Walking back to her garden
To water those trees again
Just like every other day.

# 52. Opening upto Art

Exactly
When did you stop opening up ?
what makes you feel
Everything you feel is wrong ?
This is what i ask
when i sense sad silent eyes around.

A mid age widow used to live
Around my home in my childhood
She used to shut herself
To open her heart
And cry out louder.
Some days she used to sing
But her melody is so gloomy
That it can make hearts cry.

Her story is unknown still
But when i dig deeper unto my memory
It is her gloomy melody
That says so much about
what she is going through.
Maybe our legs are too dirty
To enter her heart

And listen to what it is beating for.

One day the melody stopped
And aligned into the flowing air
I prayed for days
But what always makes me
Uncomfortable is the thought on
How many of such melodies
Do we need, in order to
Make us understand that
We need to clean ourselves
To enter someone's heart
And listen to what it is beating for ?

I am trying and still will!
I hope someday i will walk through
those slammed doors with acceptance
and listen to their gloomy melodies
Before they die in vain.

# 53. Sky carried his poems

Time,
What an aesthetic beauty you are.
We measure you with memories.
Good or Bad , You still move
He whispered looking into nothingness.

He took his journal and started writing
"If i wanted to timestamp something
I will call it as before mom and after mom"

He looked unto to the sky
And felt touched on his forehead
Brushing his hair back
While it is falling on his face again and again
He'll become that same little boy
He used to be 20 years ago
When ever he happened to sit
On the terrace.

Sky turning into orange
Makes him remember
his mother's palm with mehandi.
And that red sun,

Oh, it is her bindi.
Where as the infinity the sky holds
Is nothing but her love towards him
Till the last seconds.

He always write poems
About the beauty his mom used to carry
In her own simple ways
But was confused about narrating them.

But when will he ever knows
Sky took his poems to his mother secretly
And that's how he felt pampered back
Whenever he stares at the sky
Sitting on that terrace and writing poems.

# 54. Art of letting Go

People's interest is a muse for me
I love looking at people admiring things
In their own ways.

Sometimes i ask my grandmother
What she likes
When she say it's me
I smile back asking
So what's before my birth ?
There must be something people used to love
So deeply, that they let them go with time.

Some people say letting go
Is the hardest part of the journey
Especially when we love them most
But i think there are stories
Without harsh feelings.

Because after all Letting go is hard
When it is snached from us
But when we know
We are going to let it go
It isn't harder.

This is the truth

We Somehow neglected for centuries

Especially when we have to let go , a person or pain.

# 55. Bucket list of freedom

I met an old man
Who left nothing for himself
If he ever had something so promising
For himself,
It is nothing but his body
And a desire to live in it.

His life is so aesthetic
That it is a song
For everyone who knows singing
And a noise for others.

He walks through streets
With the words
"I would give you all the prayers I ever left for myself ".

But he wouldn't accept anything more than
The food he has to have for that day.
He had no fear to lose
And no greed to gain.

He partner is a song
And he accompanies with the bird

He talks to the fire
And campaigns along the river.

He is that breathing fairy tale
We think we can never walk through
But resides in our bucket list of freedom.

# 56. Encyclopedia of life

Old lady and life
Stories
I often search for them
Everywhere i travel
I sat alone in a railway station
And was greeted by an old lady
She talked like
There is no tomorrow
I smiled slightly,
Sliding out of
My anti social chapter

She talked about
her education back in 70s
And how she lost her husband by 80s
She talked about sending her son to the military
And on, how privileged it is
To have someone waiting for, at home.

She talked about simple things,
To run along the kite
In Order to measure its height
She talked on how to breath

And how to let it go.

She talked on how i am going
To forget the regrets
That are aching today
And how they arent even matter
few years from now.

She talked on how important
It is to lead the life
To its very end with the same curiosity
We all adopted from our mother's womb
She simply talked
And I never knew it wasn't just a talk
But an encyclopedia of life
Until i left the place and boarded the train.

# 57. Depth of a person

The metrics to measure
The depth of a person
Is to find the medium
They adopted to keep
Their soul safer.

Medium can be
Passion or existence
Sometimes together may be!
But they are contrary,
Most of the time.
Because the combination
Is situational and biased.
But when a person choose
His passion over his existence
He will turn himself into art.

People say that the art humans
Grieve over something unknown
But they aren't grieving
Because they are art humans
They are doing art
Becoz they are humans who grieve

And art adopted them closer
Like no one can.

The biggest secret about grief is
Once you settled comfortably with it
It will open your eyes towards the world
That you no longer belongs to it
You need no name , no fame
You need no race for this world grace
And you will move lighter than the air
Which dares to touch everything and anything
Without leaving the mark of interruption.

# 58. Life is a Universal Poem

Sometimes i move
Not finding answers
Because
I don't know
What to do
With the void
Inside me
Said the young poet.

Some deepest things
Never need the real answer
The old poet said.

The universe , The space
The stars , The burning sun
The moon and its love with sea
They never need the answer
And so do you
Because they all exist inside you

And to be honest
Secrets cause less destruction

And that's why the universe
Hide lots of secrets
And play hide and seek
With you most often,
In order to make the situations
Fall in their exact places
Which your soul longing
To make it happen.

Belief is beautiful
If you know the answer
You will never satisfy with it
And thus make changes
Which could destroy
Your existence.
But belief ,
it asks for your patience
Time and love
And thats how
You will appreciate the life
In the end.

Life is a universal poem
The more you understand it
The less you find it attractive
All you need to do is
Feel complexity of every phrase

And beauty of words
And it definitely not bound
To one meaning
Just seek it , you will love it.
said the old poet.

# 59. Life and Death

So Do you fear the Death ?
Lucifer asked

She looked back in silence
And said
Oh dear, I have plans on death.
It's ofcourse a boon
I never asked for!
Till it arrives.

Oh you talk like
The oldest that ever lived on the planet!
What have you seen in life ?
Lucifer questioned.

You need not see the fear
To feel the courage
And need not be the essence of the poem
To become a poet.

It happens
In the response
To your deepest understanding

Towards life.

I never asked for the life
It happened
And so the death will be
Someday!

And it is always an experience
To be both
without mixing them together
Some count days from birth
And others to the death.

But what's the point
If living in the belief of death
And dying in the greif to live
We have to live it
Like we have a life today
And vice versa!

Be Grateful for today
This hour
This minute
And This breath

# 60. For you

This is for you
To the one who face
inner conflicts.
Before outer world
Can invade

To the one who lately
Finds it hard
To shed their tears

To the one
Who have seasons
Inside their emotions
But not able to express them
Or can't control them either

To the one
Who thinks
A huge hug
Can vanish their trauma.

To the one
Who thinks they need

Validation to stop feeling unwanted.

Your strength is phenomenal
Your tears are sacred like rain water
Your emotions are poems that talks about life
You deserve all the hugs that warms the winter
You are more than world bounds on validation.
I love yaa!!